COUNTRIES IN OUR WORLD

SOUTH AFRICA
IN OUR WORLD

Ali Brownlie Bojang

A⁺
Smart Apple Media

Published by Smart Apple Media
P.O. Box 3263, Mankato, Minnesota 56002

Printed in the United States at Corporate Graphics
International in North Mankato, Minnesota.

Published by arrangement with the Watts Publishing
Group LTD, London.

Library of Congress Cataloging-in-Publication Data

Bojang, Ali Brownlie.
  South Africa in our world / Ali Brownlie Bojang.
     p. cm. -- (Countries in our world)
  Summary: "Describes the economy, government, and
  culture of South Africa today and discusses South
  Africa's influence of and relations with the rest of the
  world"--Provided by publisher.
  Includes index.
  ISBN 978-1-59920-444-4 (library binding)
  1. South Africa--Juvenile literature. I. Title.
  DT1719.B65 2011
  968.06'7--dc22
                                    2009043163

9594

Produced by: White-Thomson Publishing Ltd.

Series consultant: Rob Bowden
Editor: Sonya Newland
Designer: Hayley Cove
Picture researcher: Amy Sparks

1207
32010

9 8 7 6 5 4 3 2 1

Contents

▶ Introducing South Africa 4

▶ Landscapes and Environment 8

▶ Population and Migration 12

▶ Culture and Lifestyles 16

▶ Economy and Trade 20

▶ Government and Politics 24

▶ South Africa in 2020 28

▶ Glossary 30

▶ Further Information 31

▶ Index 32

South Africa is the eighth largest of the 53 countries in Africa. It has the largest economy and has a strong influence over what happens in other African countries. More and more, South Africa is also playing a part in global affairs.

Separated Lives

Between 1948 and 1994, South Africa had a system of government known as apartheid, which means "separateness." Although about 80 percent of the population was black, they were not allowed to vote, and white people ran the country. Under this system, black South Africans had to live in separate areas from white South Africans. They had to travel on different buses, go to different schools, and even use separate beaches and bathrooms. All around the world, people protested against apartheid.

▼ *The 1994 election was the first in which black people were allowed to vote since the beginning of apartheid in 1948.*

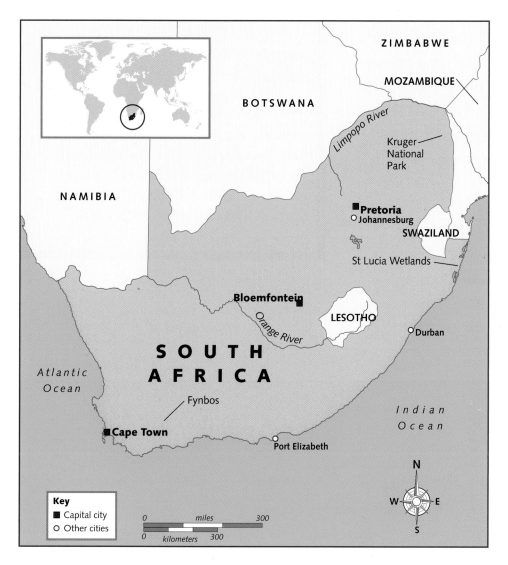

◀ *South Africa is bordered to the north by Namibia, Botswana, Zimbabwe, and Mozambique, and in the east by Swaziland. The independent kingdom of Lesotho lies completely within South Africa's borders.*

An Emerging World Power

Apartheid ended in 1994, and that year all South Africans—whatever the color of their skin—were allowed to vote. They elected their first black president, Nelson Mandela. South Africa had been banned from several international organizations and from taking part in some international sporting events because of its apartheid policy. Since 1994, however, it has been welcomed back into organizations, such as the United Nations. In 2007, it served temporarily on the UN Security Council, which decides what action to take in the event of conflict all over the world. South Africa has also improved its relationships with its neighbors in Africa, and has been a major contributor to African Union peacekeeping missions in countries such as Sudan and Burundi.

Ties Around the World

Many South Africans have family ties all over the world, reflecting the many different places from which South Africans—both black and white—originally came. As South Africa has opened up to the world, its links to other countries have strengthened in many ways. South Africa is rich in minerals, and the rapidly developing country of China, which needs lots of resources for its booming industry, has become one of South Africa's main trading partners. South Africa has global links in sporting events, too—including playing host to the 2010 soccer World Cup, attracting sports fans from all over the globe.

IT STARTED HERE

Human Ancestors

In 1998, scientists found a complete skeleton in South Africa that dated back more than three million years. It shows that some of the earliest ancestors of humans probably lived in this area.

▼ *Sports stadiums were built and other infrastructures, such as roads, were improved in preparation for the 2010 World Cup finals.*

Challenges Ahead

Although South Africa has developed a great deal in the past decade, it still faces many challenges. Just after the end of apartheid in 1995, South Africa had the highest murder rate in the world. For every 100,000 people, 67 were murdered. By 2008, this rate had dropped to 47 per 100,000 people—about the same as Washington, D.C.—but this is still one of the highest murder rates in the world.

Some black South Africans have become wealthier, but for many there are still very few jobs, low wages, poor housing conditions, and a lack of good schools. Many black South Africans are still not treated equally with white South Africans. With almost 1,000 deaths a day from HIV/AIDS, South Africa also has one of the highest death rates from the virus in the world.

▲ *These schoolchildren are enjoying a trip to the coast. The government is spending more money on education, but because of apartheid, only 14 percent of adult black South Africans today have a secondary-school education.*

BASIC DATA

Official name:	**Republic of South Africa**
Capital:	**Pretoria** (administrative capital) **Cape Town** (legislative capital) **Bloemfontein** (judicial capital)
Size:	**471,011 sq miles (1,219,912 sq km)**
Population:	**49,052,489 (2009 est.)**
Currency:	**Rand**

Landscapes and Environment

South Africa covers the southern tip of the African continent. Its longest border is with the oceans, and it stretches 1,740 miles (2,800 km). Some of the world's most diverse landscapes, animals, and plants can be found in South Africa.

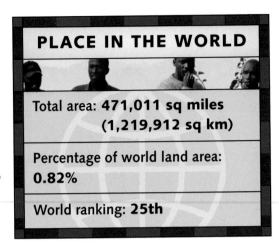

PLACE IN THE WORLD

Total area: 471,011 sq miles (1,219,912 sq km)

Percentage of world land area: 0.82%

World ranking: 25th

The High Veldt

The interior of South Africa is a huge, rolling area of grassland known as the High Veldt. This was once a massive mountain range, but over millions of years it has been worn down into a lower, smoother plateau, with an average height of 3,937 feet (1,200 m). To the north, the plateau meets the southern edge of the Kalahari Desert.

Mountains High

Mountain ranges surround the High Veldt. Along the southern edge they form a series of low ridges that run parallel to the coast. These ridges rise up in the east to form the Drakensberg ("Dragon's Back") Mountains, which contain the highest peak in South Africa —Mount Njesuthi, at 11,181 feet (3,408 m).

▼ *The Drakensberg Mountains stretch 620 miles (1,000 km) across the east side of the country.*

▲ *Nature's Valley, situated on South Africa's Garden Route—a stretch of countryside famous for its pine forests and seaside towns.*

The Beautiful South

Between the mountains and the sea lies a coastal plain. The southwest region is one of the most popular tourist destinations for both South Africans and foreign visitors. It has long, sandy beaches and pine forests. This area is also known for producing citrus fruits and wine, which are two of South Africa's main exports.

THE HOME OF...

Table Mountain

Table Mountain, near Cape Town (on cover), is thought to be one of the oldest mountains in the world. It is just over 3,281 feet (1,000 m) high and is six times older than the Himalayas in Asia.

GOING GLOBAL

South Africa has eight UNESCO World Heritage Sites—areas around the world that are considered to be of outstanding natural, historical, and cultural value. In South Africa, they include Robben Island, where Nelson Mandela was imprisoned; the fynbos; and the St. Lucia Wetlands.

▲ *Robben Island, shown here with Table Mountain in the background, is one of South Africa's eight UNESCO World Heritage Sites.*

Rivers

South Africa has two main rivers. The Orange River is the longest, rising in the Drakensberg Mountains and flowing for 1,367 miles (2,200 km) across the country to the Atlantic Ocean. South Africa's second longest river, the Limpopo, flows eastward into the Indian Ocean, and forms the border between South Africa and Zimbabwe.

Flora of the Fynbos

The fynbos is a unique area in the Cape region of South Africa. With nearly 8,000 different species, it has the highest concentration of plants in the world, many of which cannot be found anywhere else on the planet. Fynbos means "fine bush," and the area was given this name because many of the plants are evergreen with fine, needle-like leaves.

Climate

Most of South Africa has a moderate climate, which means it is neither too hot nor too cold. On the High Veldt, summers are warm and winters are cool—sometimes freezing. The east coast has almost a tropical climate, which means it is warm and wet. Summer temperatures are on average around 75°F (24°C), and winter temperatures are around 64°F (18°C). In the east rainfall is high—around 39 inches (1,000 mm) a year. However, this gradually decreases further west, to less than 5 inches (130 mm). The west often suffers from droughts, and because this is the main crop-farming region in South Africa, there can be food shortages and people's livelihoods can be threatened.

IT'S A FACT!

The Vredefort Dome in South Africa is the largest meteorite crash site in the world. It was formed two billion years ago. Some scientists believe that the impact could have increased the Earth's oxygen levels, allowing life forms to develop.

▼ *Kruger National Park is one of the world's largest wildlife sanctuaries. Savannah and dense bush make it an ideal home for elephants and many other animals.*

Population and Migration

South Africa's population is made up of so many different ethnic groups that it has been nicknamed the "rainbow nation." Over thousands of years, people have moved to South Africa from countries all over the world.

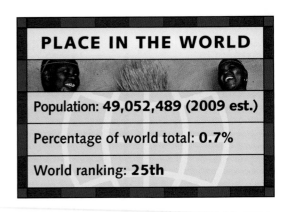
Who are South Africans?

Black Africans make up nearly 80 percent of the total population. The rest of the South African population is made up of white people, people of Asian origin, and mixed race people.

▼ *Black and white South African students mix at Cape Town university.*

Where Do They Live?

Nearly 21 percent of South Africans live in KwaZulu-Natal province. Gauteng province, containing the largest city, Johannesburg, and the administrative capital, Pretoria, is the smallest but most densely populated province. Although the Northern Cape covers nearly 30 percent of the country's land area, only 2.3 percent of the population lives there.

▲ *An HIV-positive patient is shown how to schedule the drugs she must take. This clinic in Cape Town is run by the international organization Doctors Without Borders.*

Growing Population

The HIV/AIDS virus seriously affects the growth and life expectancy of South Africa's population. Although the population is growing, the rate of growth has slowed down considerably in the past 20 years. In the 1980s, the rate of growth was 2.4 percent, but by 2008 this had fallen to 0.8 percent. The average life expectancy has also fallen, and is now at 49 years. It is estimated that without HIV/AIDS, the average life expectancy would be about 15 years more.

IT'S A FACT!

South Africa has the worst AIDS epidemic in the world. At the end of 2007, there were about 5.7 million people living with the HIV virus. Of these, 280,000 were under the age of 15. It is estimated that South Africa has about 1.4 million children who have lost at least one parent to the disease.

Moving to South Africa

Over the past 100 years, many people have moved to South Africa. In the 1930s and 1940s, Jewish refugees from Eastern Europe, fleeing from persecution in their own countries, sought refuge in South Africa. Later—throughout the 1970s and 1980s—many people from the United Kingdom settled in South Africa, as well as people from China and Portugal. Since the end of apartheid in the 1990s, the majority of immigrants have come from Nigeria as well as parts of Asia, Europe, and the United States.

Refugees from Zimbabwe

It is thought that over a million Zimbabwean refugees, fleeing from poverty and conflict in their own country, crossed the border to South Africa in 2008. Some of them entered the country illegally and if they were caught, these people were sent back to Zimbabwe. There were so many refugees that some people in South Africa were afraid that they would start taking houses and jobs that they felt belonged to South Africans. There were several attacks on Zimbabweans and other immigrants as a result.

▼ *In 2008, violence increased against immigrants, and many left the country. These people are waiting to board buses to Mozambique.*

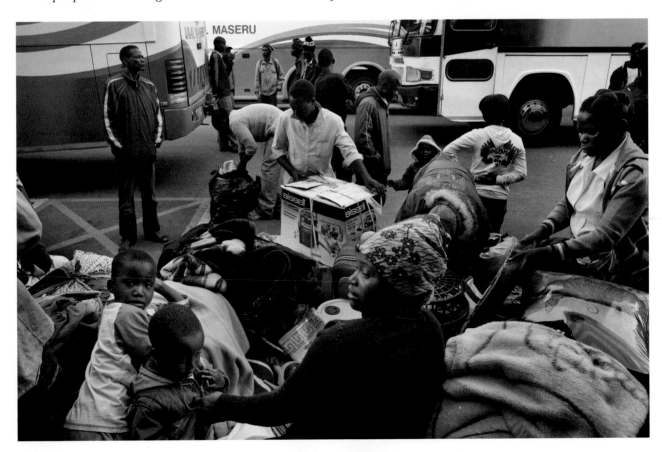

City Living

During apartheid, black people were forced to live in rural areas, known as "homelands." Men left their families to find work in the cities—even though this was often illegal—and lived in settlements set aside for them known as townships. This flow of people to South Africa's cities has continued, but today it is not illegal and people can move wherever they like. Black people are moving into areas of cities where once only white people lived. Today, nearly 60 percent of South Africans live in cities, and urban areas are growing rapidly.

GOING GLOBAL

Many young, skilled people, such as IT professionals, doctors, dentists, scientists, nurses, and teachers, have left South Africa. They go looking for better-paid jobs in other countries such as the UK, the U.S., and Canada, as well as other African countries. South Africa needs to find a way to persuade skilled people to stay, since they have an important contribution to make to their country's future.

▼ *As more and more people move to the cities for work, townships like this are spreading further out, expanding urban areas.*

Culture and Lifestyles

South Africa's music, dance, literature, art, and drama have all been influenced by a mixture of African, European, and Asian cultures. Like many other countries, modern popular culture in South Africa is also strongly influenced by the United States and Europe.

GOING GLOBAL

During apartheid, many people living in the townships created art about their lives. Business people and diplomats took many of these paintings out of the country to the U.S., the UK, Australia, and Canada. South Africans are now trying to get these pictures back, as they are an important part of their country's history.

Traditional Art

Some of the earliest art in the world can be found in South Africa. During the Stone Age—up to 35,000 years ago—the Kohl and San bush people lived in the Drakensberg Mountains. They made cave paintings showing what their daily lives were like, often depicting hunting and battles. Some of these paintings can still be seen today.

◀ *This rock art depicting a battle scene was painted on a cave wall in the Drakensberg Mountains thousands of years ago.*

▲ *South African music and dance draws from many different influences. This is a Zulu tribal dance.*

Music Mixture

Two popular forms of South African music, jazz and gospel, originated with West African slaves brought over by European settlers. Young people have developed their own style of music, known as *kwaito*. This is a mixture of hip-hop, R&B, raga, and techno music.

Religion

About 80 percent of South Africans are Christians, although many black South Africans combine traditional African and Christian beliefs. Other religions include Hinduism, Islam, and Judaism.

FAMOUS SOUTH AFRICAN

Miriam Makeba (1932–2008)

Miriam Makeba was a singer and human rights activist. She was exiled from South Africa because she spoke out against the policy of apartheid, but she used her singing and concerts around the world to draw international attention to the campaign against apartheid in her country.

Exporting South African Culture

Over the years, many people have left South Africa, either to settle or to work for a few years. They often take with them things that remind them of their home country. One example of this is *biltong*—a kind of dried meat first brought to South Africa by Dutch settlers. Now it is stocked in shops all over the world in countries where South Africans have settled, and is popular with non-South Africans, too.

▼ *These men are making biltong, a South African snack of dried meat that is now eaten all over the world.*

The Media

Until 1975, there was no television in South Africa because the government did not want South Africans to know what was happening in other countries. Today, many of the programs people watch are the same as those in Europe or North America, including the South African versions of *Big Brother* and *Dancing with the Stars*. The most popular soap opera in South Africa is *Soul City*, which tackles subjects such as HIV/AIDS. It is now being broadcast in neighboring countries such as Botswana and Zimbabwe.

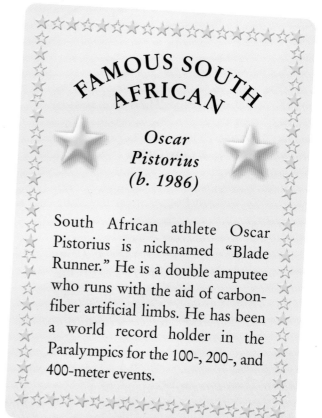

◀ Rugby star Bryan Habana helped South Africa win the World Cup in 2007, and was named Player of the Year by the International Rugby Board.

FAMOUS SOUTH AFRICAN

Oscar Pistorius (b. 1986)

South African athlete Oscar Pistorius is nicknamed "Blade Runner." He is a double amputee who runs with the aid of carbon-fiber artificial limbs. He has been a world record holder in the Paralympics for the 100-, 200-, and 400-meter events.

Sports

South Africa is a great sporting nation, and some people believe sports help bring all the different races of South Africa together. However, white and black people still tend to play different sports. White people tend to play cricket and rugby, while black people tend to play soccer. South Africa was not allowed to take part in some sporting events during apartheid, but since then, South African teams have been successful in international events, particularly rugby. The South African rugby team won the World Cup in 2007. In cricket, too, the national team has performed well. South Africa hosted the Cricket World Cup in 2003, and it reached the semi-finals in 2007.

Economy and Trade

Since the end of apartheid, South Africa's economy has developed rapidly because it has been able to increase its trade with other countries. However, around 4.5 million people in South Africa still live on less than $2 a day.

IT'S A FACT!

South Africa has the 25th largest economy in the world. It produces more goods than Portugal, Russia, or Singapore. It also has Africa's biggest economy—three times larger than Nigeria or Egypt.

A Growing Economy

South Africa has the most important economy in Africa. It has good road and railroad networks with other countries in southern Africa, as well as connections to the rest of the world. The end of apartheid meant that foreign companies started to invest in South Africa, and because of this, the country's economy has grown steadily. The value of all the goods and services produced in South Africa increased by 2.7 percent in 2001. By 2007, it had grown by 5.1 percent.

▼ *South African grapes are exported and enjoyed all over the world. Some are made into wine.*

Natural Resources

South Africa's wealth is in its natural resources. Nearly 90 percent of all the platinum on Earth can be found in South Africa, as well as 80 percent of the manganese, 73 percent of the chrome, and 41 percent of the gold. There are still many more mineral deposits waiting to be exploited. South Africa is the world's third-largest producer of diamonds, and these precious stones are sent to Antwerp in Belgium and Amsterdam in the Netherlands to be cut into jewels and for other purposes.

GLOBAL LEADER

The world's largest diamond was found in South Africa in 1905. It was cut into two large diamonds and 104 smaller ones, and these now form part of the British Crown Jewels.

Trading Partners

South Africa trades most with the UK, the U.S., Germany, Italy, Belgium, China, and Japan. Trade with other African countries is increasing. Its biggest exports are gold, diamonds, metals and minerals, machinery, and equipment, as well as agricultural goods such as fruit, flowers, and livestock. South Africa's seasons are opposite of Europe's, so it is able to supply food when it is out of season there. It imports machinery, chemicals, petroleum products, and scientific equipment.

◀ *This woman is working in a factory in Durban. Manufacturing is vital to South Africa's economy, which produces machinery and equipment that are sold overseas.*

Relationship with China

South Africa has benefited from the economic growth of China, and it is now China's largest trading partner in Africa. Between 2007 and 2008, there was a 62 percent growth in trade between China and Africa, and trade with South Africa made up the largest part of that. South Africa exports iron ore, copper, chrome, timber, and paper pulp to China, and imports goods such as toys and electronic equipment.

GOING GLOBAL

South Africa is becoming a popular choice for international businesses to set up call centers. It has the advantages of being in more or less the same time zone as Europe, and between that of the Americas and Asia, and there are many English-speaking South Africans looking for work.

Energy

South Africa uses coal to generate most of its electricity, and the emissions from power plants make it the fourteenth highest producer of greenhouse gases in the world. The country is now trying to reduce its emissions, and alternative energy sources are being considered, such as nuclear power and natural gas, as well as forms of renewable energy, such as wind and solar power.

▼ *Sasol is the world's first—and largest— oil-from-coal refinery. It provides 40 percent of the country's fuel.*

Tourism

Tourism is one of South Africa's fastest-growing industries, and in 2008 it was worth US$8.3 billion. The number of foreign tourists increases every year—in 2007 there were around 9 million. Tourism has created many jobs. People visit to enjoy the good weather, the beautiful scenery, and the wildlife they can see in the national parks and game reserves. Some tourists are interested in South Africa's recent history and tour townships such as Soweto. Tourists come from other countries in Africa as well as North America, the UK, Russia, Hungary, Finland, India, Japan, Thailand, and Singapore.

▲ *Every year, millions of tourists visit South Africa to see sights such as the penguin colonies on Boulder Beach near Cape Town.*

IT'S A FACT!

In 2008, the government announced a plan to improve the economy of the township of Soweto by investing in shops, theaters, and other entertainment venues to try to attract even more tourists to the area.

Government and Politics

South Africa experiences many of the same economic and social problems as other African countries. However, because of its recent history, it can help promote democracy in other African nations.

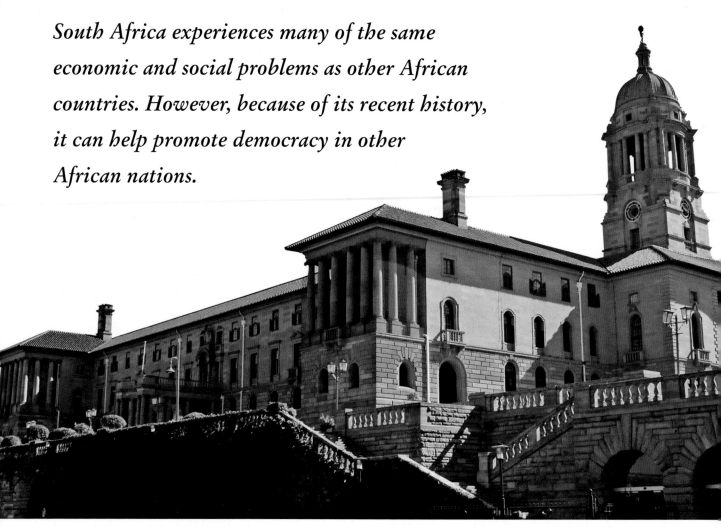

▲ *The Union Buildings in Pretoria are the official seat of the South African government.*

Rejoining the World

One of the most important jobs for the new government in 1994 was to reestablish relationships with other countries. South Africa is now part of the African Union (AU) once more, and is an active member of the United Nations. South Africa is also becoming more involved with the G20 group of countries, as it is recognized as a nation with global importance. The South African government has also established a partnership with the European Union.

IT'S A FACT!

Pretoria has the second largest number of foreign embassies in the world. Only Washington, D.C., has more.

The Parliamentary System

Each province in South Africa has its own provincial government, which is responsible for local matters such as health care and education. Each province sends 10 representatives to the national parliament and elections are held in South Africa every five years. In 2008, Kgalema Motlanthe became the third president of the new South Africa, replacing Thabo Mbeki—who had succeeded Nelson Mandela.

GLOBAL LEADER

Dismantling Nuclear Weapons

In the early 1990s, South Africa became the only country in the world to voluntarily get rid of its nuclear weapons. Since then, South Africa's leaders have tried to persuade other countries to do the same.

Community Projects

There are many small community projects in South Africa that help those in need. Many of these are funded by overseas aid organizations. One such project, Fancy Stitch, supports women by bringing them together to make brightly colored handcrafts, artwork, and textiles. The women create works that say something about their lives, such as HIV/AIDS, farming, livestock, cities, families, gardens, work, and wildlife. They sell their products to bring in much-needed money.

▼ *Women from the Ndebele tribe sell their handcrafts to a tourist outside a craft shop at a cultural village near Johannesburg.*

Developing Democracy

South Africa has demonstrated to the rest of Africa how a democracy can work. In contrast to the apartheid years, it now has a constitution that bans any form of discrimination. However, one party—the African National Congress (ANC)—dominates the government. Other major political parties represented in Parliament are the Congress of the People, which split from the ANC, and the Inkatha Freedom Party, which mainly represents Zulu voters.

Peacekeeping

South Africa has been called on to take part in peacekeeping missions in several African countries. It has sent troops to the Democratic Republic of Congo (DRC), Sudan, and Burundi. In 2008, along with many other countries, South Africa called for a ceasefire in the DRC so that aid could reach the refugees. Members of the government have also played a key role in trying to arrange peace talks between political parties, particularly in South Africa's neighboring country Zimbabwe.

▼ *Former president Thabo Mbeki inspects South African troops sent to Sudan to help restore peace in the region in 2005.*

Problems for the Government

Much has improved in South Africa, but it still faces many problems. The fact that there is still a big divide between rich and poor causes unrest, resentment, and crime, which is particularly bad in the big cities. The HIV/AIDS epidemic makes this situation even worse, because money that could be used to develop the country is spent instead on caring for those with the virus.

▼ *Nelson Mandela meets children in 2005 after visiting the museum that has been opened at Robben Island, where he was imprisoned.*

FAMOUS SOUTH AFRICAN

Nelson Mandela (b. 1918)

Nelson Mandela was imprisoned in 1964 for campaigning against apartheid. He remained there for 27 years, but after his release he was elected president of South Africa. He retired in 1999 and since then he has been an ambassador for many causes, such as HIV/AIDS and poverty in Africa.

South Africa is likely to change even more rapidly between now and 2020 than it has in recent years. The changes that have been made since the end of apartheid have brought prosperity for some people, but South Africa still faces some challenges.

A Modern Country

Experts believe that by 2020, the number of people living in cities in South Africa could be as high as 80 percent of the population. This means that services such as water supply and transportation will need to be provided for all these people. There will be a lot of pressure on the government to provide these, as well as ensuring that there is enough housing and enough jobs for everyone.

▼ *As more people move to cities such as Durban, more housing, better public transportation, and better health care will be needed.*

Climate Change

Climate change could have a big impact on South Africa in the next few years. Existing plants and animals would find it difficult to adapt to rising temperatures. Some species in South Africa's famous Kruger National Park are already dying out. Higher temperatures would mean there is less rain, which could reduce crop production.

▲ *Schools in South Africa are now integrated, and accept both black and white students. It is important for black South Africans to be treated equally if the country is to develop.*

GLOBAL LEADER

Hospitals

The largest hospital in Africa is in the township of Soweto. Every day, more than 2,000 patients check into Baragwanath Hospital. Nearly half of them are HIV positive.

Development for All

The major issue of inequality must be tackled in the near future. As the economy grows, and more people move from the country to towns and cities, the government needs to ensure that money is spent on schools, housing, and hospitals so that people can be lifted out of poverty, which is at the heart of most of South Africa's problems. Unless this happens, unrest will continue.

Growing Equality

Although black people and white people still tend to lead fairly separate lives, it is likely that in the future there will be more mixed schools, businesses, government, and sports. South Africa's problems will be helped if the economy continues to develop and everyone benefits from the new wealth. These changes will all help South Africa become a richer and more globally important country in the future.

Glossary

African Union an international organization that promotes unity, cooperation, and solidarity among African states.

ANC the African National Congress—the main political party in South Africa, based on the first liberation movement.

constitution a document that lays out the main laws of a nation. Laws are not allowed to be passed that contradict a country's constitution.

continents the Earth's seven great land masses—Africa, Antarctica, Asia, Australia, Europe, North America, and South America.

democracy a form of government in which people vote for the leaders they wish to represent them.

drought a water shortage caused by a long spell with little or no rain.

economy the financial system of a country or region, including how much money is made from the production and sale of goods and services.

export to transport products or materials abroad for sale or trade.

G20 a group of countries (Canada, France, Germany, Italy, Japan, Russia, the United Kingdom, and the United States), that meets to discuss global economic concerns.

homelands under apartheid, areas set aside for the black African population.

immigrant a person who has moved to another country to live.

import to bring in goods or materials from a foreign country for sale.

minerals solid substances, such as limestone or quartz, that occur naturally within the earth.

national park an area of land that has been declared public property by a government in order to preserve both the land and the wildlife that lives on it.

plateau an area of high, flat land.

refugee someone who has had to flee from their own country because of war or persecution.

resources things that are available to use, often to help develop a country's industry and economy. Resources could be minerals, workers (labor), or water.

township a settlement on the outskirts of many major South African cities.

veldt a wide-open area of countryside.

wetland an area of marshy land.

Further Information

Books

Cape Town
by Rob Bowden
(Chelsea House Publishers, 2006)

The Release of Nelson Mandela
by Kate Riggs
(Creative Education, 2010)

Teens in South Africa
by David Seidman
(Compass Point Books, 2009)

Apartheid in South Africa.
by Michael J. Martin
(Lucent Books, 2006)

The African Union
by Russell Roberts
(Mason Crest Publishers, 2008)

Countries in the News:
South Africa
by Senker, Cathy
(Smart Apple Media, 2008)

Web Sites

https://www.cia.gov/library/publications/
the-world-factbook/geos/sf.html
Facts and statistics about South Africa.

http://www.southafrica.net
South Africa's official tourism page that includes
pictures, interactive maps, and lots of details about
kite boarding and other cultural recreation.

http://www.nelsonmandela.org/index.php/memory/
views/biography
A fascinating biography of South Africa's most
famous statesman.

Every effort has been made by the publisher to ensure
that these web sites contain no inappropriate or offensive
material. However, because of the nature of the Internet,
it is impossible to guarantee that the contents of these sites
will not be altered. We strongly advise that Internet access
is supervised by a responsible adult.

Index

Numbers in **bold** indicate pictures.

A

African National Congress 26
African Union 5, 24
animals 8, **11**, 23, 28
apartheid 4, 5, 7, 14, 15, 16, 17, 19, 20, 26, 27, 28
art 16, **16**, 25
Asia 9, 12, 14, 16, 22

B

biltong 18, **18**
Burundi 5, 26

C

Canada 15, 16
Cape Town 9, **12**, 23
China 6, 14, 21, 22
climate 11, 28
community projects 25, **25**

D

dance **17**
democracy 24, 25, 26
Democratic Republic of Congo 26
diamonds 21
Drakensberg Mountains 8, **8**, 10, 16
Durban 21, **28**

E

economy 4, 20, 21, 22, 23, 24, 29
energy 22
equality 7, 29
Europe 14, 16, 17, 18, 21, 22, 24
exports 9, 20, 21, 22

F

farming 11, 25
fynbos 10

G

gold 21, **21**
government 7, 18, 24, 25, 26, 28, 29

H

Habana, Bryan **19**
High Veldt 8, 11
HIV/AIDS 7, 13, **13**, 18, 25, 27, **27**, 29
housing 7, 28, 29

I

immigrants 14, **14**
imports 21, 22

J

jobs 7, 15, 23, 28
Johannesburg 12, 25

K

Kalahari Desert 8
Kruger National Park **11**, 28

L

life expectancy 13

M

Makeba, Miriam 17
Mandela, Nelson 5, 10, 25, 27
Mbeki, Thabo 25, **26**
minerals 6, 21
Motlanthe, Kgalema 25
music 16, 17

N

natural resources 21
Nigeria 14, 20
nuclear weapons 25

P

peacekeeping missions 5, 26, **26**
Pistorius, Oscar 19

plants 8, 10, 28
population 4, 7, 12, 13, 28
poverty 14, 27, 29
Pretoria 12, 24, **24**

R

refugees 14, 26
religion 17
rivers 10
Robben Island 10, **10**, 27
Russia 20, 23

S

schools 4, 7, **7**, 29, **29**
Singapore 20, 23
Soweto 23, 29
sports 5, 6, **6**, 19, **19**, 29
Sudan 5, 26, **26**

T

Table Mountain 9, **10**
tourism 9, 23, 25
townships 15, **15**, 16, 23, 29
trade 6, 20, 21, 22

U

United Kingdom 14, 15, 16, 21, 23
United Nations 5, 24
United States 7, 14, 15, 16, 18, 21, 23, 24

V

voting 4, **4**, 5, 25, 26
Vredefort Dome 11

W

wine 9, **20**
World Heritage Sites 10, **10**

Z

Zimbabwe 5, 10, 14, 18, 26